ADRENALIN RUSH

SKATEBOARDING

JACKSON TELLER

This edition published in 2013 by
Franklin Watts
338 Euston Road
London NW1 3BH

Franklin Watts Australia
Level 17/207 Kent Street
Sydney NSW 2000

Produced by Tall Tree Ltd

A CIP catalogue record for this book is available from the British Library.

Dewey Classification: 796.2'2

ISBN: 978 1 4451 1842 0

Printed in China

Franklin Watts is a division of Hachette Children's Books, an Hachette UK company.

www.hachette.co.uk

Picture credits:
t–top, b–bottom, l–left, r–right, c–centre
front cover Steven Robertson/istockphoto, back cover Monkey Business Images/Dreamstime.com, 1 Matthew Benoit/Dreamstime.com, 4b Forest Woodward/istockphoto.com, 4–5 Rick Becker-leckrone/Dreamstime.com, 6–7 TobiasK/Wikkicommons, 7bl Ted Soqui/Corbis, 8 Jorg Hackemann/Dreamstime.com, 9tr Gustavo Fernandes/Dreamstime.com, 9b Fernando Mafra/Wikicommons, 10 Amandamhanna/Dreamstime.com, 11tr Josef Muellek/Dreamstime.com, 11b Steve Collender/Shutterstock, 12 Galina Barskaya/Dreamstime.com, 13tl Marcio Eugenio/Dreamstime.com, 13c Gravityimaging/Dreamstime.com, 13b Peter Kim/Dreamstime.com, 14 Charles Knox/Dreamstime.com, 15t Anthony Hall/Dreamstime.com, 16–17 Galina Barskaya/Dreamstime.com, 17tr Matthew Benoit/Dreamstime.com, 17br Chad Santos/Wikicommons, 18–19 Jfitch/GNU, 19br ESPN, 19tr Rick Rickman/NewSport/Corbis, 20 Jose Gil/Dreamstime.com, 21tr Warren Goldswain/Shutterstock, 21bl Getty Images, 22bl adrienne miller/istockphoto.com 22–23 Sam Gordon of Pavel Skates, 24–25 Stefan Kubitschek, 25c Dominick Mauro Jr/Shutterstock.com, 26 Steven Robertson/istock, 27tr plastique/Shutterstock, 28–29 Steve Boyle/Corbis, 28br Jorchr/GNU

Disclaimer
The website addresses (URLs) included in this book were valid at the time of going to press. However, because of the nature of the Internet, it is possible that some addresses have changed, or sites may have changed or closed down since publication. While the author and publisher regret any inconvenience this may cause to readers, no responsibility for any such changes can be accepted either by the author or the publisher.

In preparation of this book, all due care has been exercised with regard to the advice, activities and techniques depicted. The publishers regret that they can accept no liability for any loss or injury sustained. When learning a new activity, it is important to get expert tuition and to follow a manufacturer's instructions.

Words in **bold** are in the glossary on page 30.

CONTENTS

'Hitting the concrete' does not mean actually hitting or **slamming** into the concrete (though you probably will at some point). It means going out skateboarding. Ever since it first appeared, skateboarding has been hugely popular. This book will show you why.

The joy of skating

It takes time to learn how to skate. It can take hours and hours of practice to get a move right, and you are guaranteed to have picked up a few scrapes and bruises by the time you know how to do it. So why is skateboarding so popular?

The joy of skating is that you can learn at your own pace and in your own way. No one pushes you – there are no coaches shouting advice, no parents looking on. There is always a new trick to learn and the satisfaction of finally **landing** it makes the struggle worthwhile.

An old-school downhill longboarder 'hangs ten', with all ten toes dangling over the nose of his skateboard.

Skater world

If you are a skater, you can find somewhere to skate in almost any city in the world. Europe and North America are real hotbeds of skating, but from Rio de Janeiro to Tokyo, there are skaters **ripping it up** in skate parks, on ramps and in the streets.

A timeless move, as this diamond-pattern-crazy skater launches off the lip of a skate park bowl.

Three top skate movies
- The Search For Animal Chin – *a 1980s skate classic, with a great, cheesy storyline.*
- Birdhouse: The Beginning – *features one of the best skater lineups ever, including Tony Hawk, Willy Santos and Shaun White.*
- Es Menimaki – *inspiring riding from a crew that constantly pushes the boundaries of what you can do on a skateboard.*

The first skaters were surfers. One day in the 1950s, somewhere on the coast of California, there were no waves. A bored surfer pulled his sister's roller skates apart and nailed the wheels to an old bit of plank. He had made the first skateboard.

*This sequence shows a flatland **ollie**. The skater jumps up while snapping the tail of the board down and sliding the front foot forwards.*

The sidewalk surfers

Other surfers quickly spotted that these new contraptions were a great way to practise their surfing skills. Pretty soon the pavements were full of kids rattling along 'sidewalk surfing', as the new activity was known. The craze spread like wildfire, and by the 1960s skateboarding had become a multi-million dollar industry.

The ollie takes off

The mid-1970s were an important time for skateboarding. In California, USA, skaters had started riding drained swimming pools, inventing a new school of skating in the process. In Florida, USA, Adam Gelfand came up with a way of jumping his board without using his hands. This became known as the ollie, and it is the basis for many skating tricks.

Stacy Peralta comes from Venice Beach, California. At 15 he started skating for the legendary Zephyr skate team. Four years later, he was ranked as the world's best skater. Peralta is now a television and movie director. His best-known movies are *Dogtown and Z-Boys* (2001), which charts the skateboarding revolution of the 1970s, and *Riding Giants* (2004), which is about big-wave surfing.

STACY PERALTA

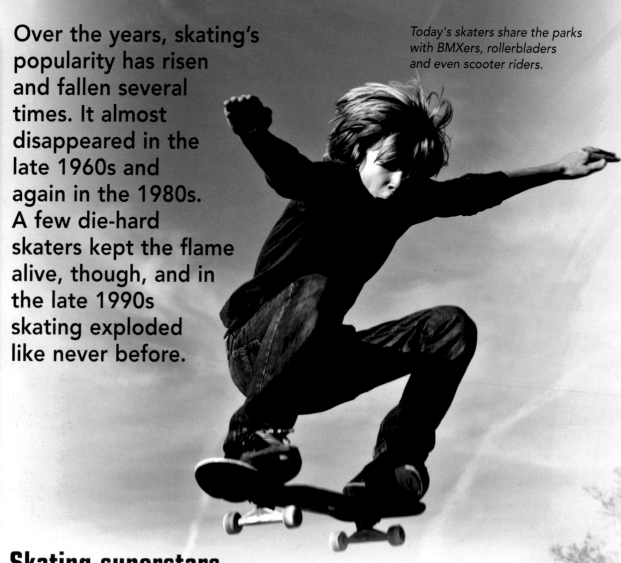

Over the years, skating's popularity has risen and fallen several times. It almost disappeared in the late 1960s and again in the 1980s. A few die-hard skaters kept the flame alive, though, and in the late 1990s skating exploded like never before.

Today's skaters share the parks with BMXers, rollerbladers and even scooter riders.

Skating superstars

Skateboarding grew in popularity partly because the best skaters started performing mind-blowing tricks. Probably the top skater of the time – or ever – was Tony Hawk. His 900-degree spin at the 1999 X-Games is still one of skating's most famous moments. Only three other skaters pulled off a **900** in competition over the next ten years.

A competitor at the Best Trick Championship in Caldas da Rainha, Portugal, practises a move before his round of the contest.

Skateboarding today

After learning the basics of getting the board moving and steering it, most riders decide that they prefer one of these different styles of skating:

- ramp skating – this has the potential for high-speed aerials.

- street skating – this features a huge variety of technical ollies and **grinds**.

- longboarding – skaters cruise around, with the odd high-speed slide thrown in for fun.

- flatland – skaters pull off amazing tricks on smooth, level surfaces.

Ban this dangerous activity! *Skateboarding was banned in Norway between 1978 and 1989. It was thought to be too dangerous. Skaters were forced underground: they had to build ramps deep in the woods and practise on boards imported from abroad.*

Bob Burnquist is a Brazilian-American skater who **turned pro** at just 14. He is famous for making difficult tricks even harder, then pulling them off! In 2010, he became the first skater to land a **fakie**-to-fakie 900 – which means he took off and landed going backwards.

There are so many different kinds of skateboard, it can make your head spin. Even so, the basic parts of every board have been the same since skating was invented: wheels, trucks, a deck and grip tape.

The ideal board

You can choose to buy a fully made skateboard, called a complete, or you can build one yourself once you have the individual pieces. Either way, it is a good idea to go to a skate shop to ask for advice.

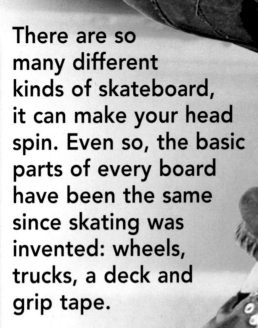

Trucks
These allow the board to turn when the rider leans to one side of the board or the other. The width of the truck always matches the width of the deck.

Bearings
These fit between the wheels and the truck axle, and let the wheels spin.

Wheels
Bigger, softer wheels roll better, while smaller, harder ones are good for tricks. Wheel hardness is given as a durometer number: 95 is hard; 85 is soft.

Grip tape
Helps your feet to grip on the deck.

Deck
The part on which you stand. The deck is always made of wood, usually with a kicktail (slight flip) at the front and back.

This street deck has been pretty well used: the nose has been bashed about and the wheels look like they are just about used up. Time for a new one!

Types of skateboard

Street boards, pool boards, slalom boards, longboards, downhill boards… there are many types of skateboard, but the two main kinds are:

• street boards – these are the standard board. They are usually about 75 centimetres long and 18–20 centimetres wide. The wheels are small, hard and light. This makes tricks easier, but the boards do not roll well.

• longboards – these can be anything from 90–150 centimetres long, and a little wider than street boards. The wheels are softer and bigger and mounted on wider trucks. This allows the rider to roll along easily, carving out big, swooping turns.

Longboard skateboards, such as this one, can be twice the length of a normal street board.

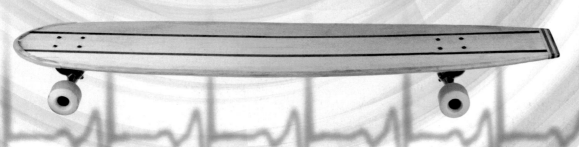

Helmet
The right fit is very important – helmets must not be loose. The straps need to fit snugly, and be done up all the time.

Elbow pads
Both elbow pads and knee pads need to fit tight enough not to slip down, but not so tight that they stop you from moving.

Kneepads
*Experienced **vert** skaters learn to land on their kneepads when they fall off, and slide harmlessly down the ramp.*

Shoes
*Classic skate shoes have flat soles. This gives them good **traction** against the grip tape on the deck.*

Aside from a board, not much extra equipment is needed for skateboarding. Some skate parks will not let you ride without a helmet, but for vert skating people usually wear one anyway. Most skaters add knee and elbow pads, too, as these are the bits of your body on which you usually land in a fall.

Skate clothing and other gear

Most skaters prefer loose clothing and flat-soled shoes. They rarely wear many layers, because skating is hot work. Shorts, baggy jeans or trousers, and a T-shirt or hooded top are usually most comfortable. Other useful things to have include:

Downhill skaters reach extremely high speeds, so full leathers are essential if you want to have skin on your back after a fall!

• rucksack – for extra clothes, water and a phone.

• skate tool – for tightening up trucks and wheels.

Longboarders do not usually wear pads or helmets. A pair of tough gloves does come in handy if you are doing a slide, though!

Shaun White is sometimes called the Flying Tomato because of his red hair. As well as being an Olympic gold medallist at snowboarding in 2006 and 2010, Shaun has won medals for skating at the X-Games. White is the only skater ever to land a frontside heelflip 540 body variable – a trick so complicated it makes your nose bleed just to think about it.

It sounds odd, but street skating does not always happen on the street. Skating is not allowed in some urban areas. Even where it is, there is always the risk you will scare, annoy, injure or get shouted at by a member of the public.

A big ollie – with an extra flip or two thrown in – gets this skater airborne in style.

Skate-park street skating

One of the best places for a bit of street skating action, whether you want to watch it or do it, is a skate park. Most parks have 'street' areas. These are filled with the kind of opportunities for tricks you would find on a real street, only better! In a park, there are no pedestrians or security guards – just other skaters.

Preparing to land after a board slide on a lovely, smooth metal rail.

Street obstacles

Street skaters perform their tricks using whatever obstacles they find. Lots of these are reproduced inside skate parks:

- stairs – one of the most spectacular street tricks is a stair jump. The skater ollies from the top to the bottom of the stairs, without touching any steps.

- handrails – used to grind along, skaters slide the deck or trucks along the handrails before jumping off.

- blocks and kerbs – like handrails, these are used for grinds.

Many skate parks also have 'fun boxes'. These are four ramps that meet in a flat top and provide a launch pad for all kinds of tricks.

The first contest
The first 'street style' contest was held in San Francisco's Golden Gate Park in 1983. An amateur local rider named Tommy Guerrero won. You can check out his relaxed style in the classic movies Future Primitive *and* The Search For Animal Chin.

KNOW THE FACTS

A good ramp rider always draws a crowd.
And no wonder: ramp skating is electrifyingly
exciting, even if you are only watching!
It can be heart-poundingly scary when
you are actually skating – especially when
things go wrong!

Mini ramps

Injuries are common in ramp skating, some of them serious.
Most skaters build up their skills and confidence on a mini
ramp before moving on to larger ones. Mini ramps are usually
less than 2 metres high. On a ramp this size, crashes are not
likely to be really serious. This is where most skaters learn
the basics of ramp riding:

- dropping in – the moment when you
  start a run by plunging down the ramp,
  from the platform at the top.

- pumping – using the slope of the
  ramp, your body weight and the
  movement of your hips and legs
  to build up speed.

- transitioning – changing from
  going up the ramp to coming
  back down it.

Not a great idea:
2 skaters + 1 ramp =
crash waiting to happen.

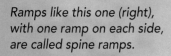

Ramps like this one (right), with one ramp on each side, are called spine ramps.

Speed machines

Mini ramps are not just for beginners. Even on a small ramp, a skilful skater can generate some real speed. And because the ramp is smaller, the skater has less time between tricks. Under the feet of a good skater, a mini ramp is a platform for a stream of lightning-fast, highly tricky moves, which can leave an audience open-mouthed in amazement.

Cheese and crackers
Are you hungry for some top mini ramp action? Have a look at the Cheese and Crackers DVD. It stars two of the world's best mini ramp riders: Chris Haslam and Daewon Song.

ON THE SCREEN

17

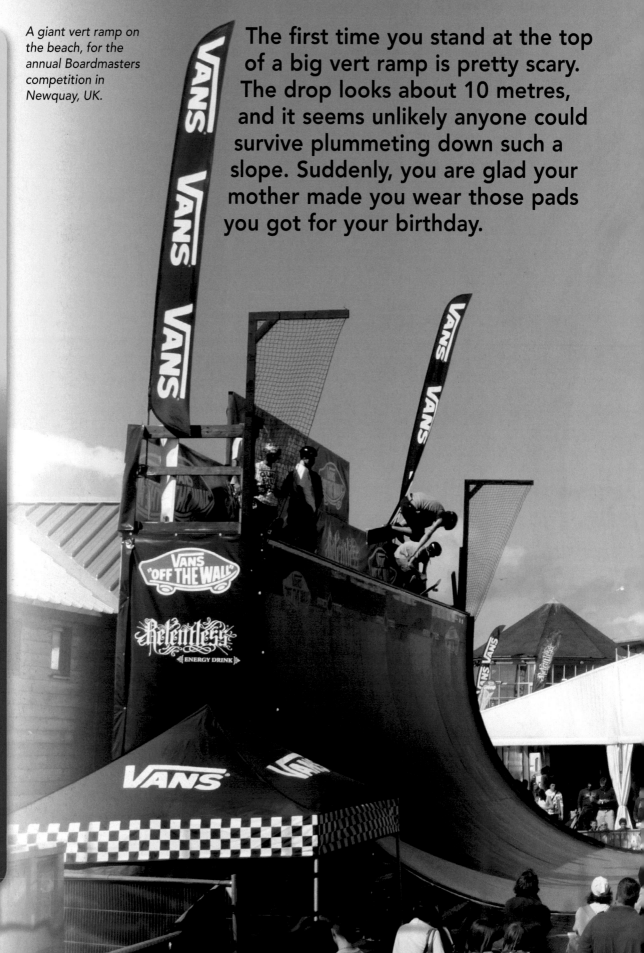

A giant vert ramp on the beach, for the annual Boardmasters competition in Newquay, UK.

The first time you stand at the top of a big vert ramp is pretty scary. The drop looks about 10 metres, and it seems unlikely anyone could survive plummeting down such a slope. Suddenly, you are glad your mother made you wear those pads you got for your birthday.

Vert = vertical = good

People DO survive their first go on a vert ramp, and most come back for another turn. The vertical walls on a vert ramp mean that you can launch straight up into the air, instead of having to ollie yourself vertical as you would on a mini-ramp.

Mega ramps

In 2003, Danny Way landed a world-record air that took him 7.2 metres above the top of the ramp. You can bet that straight away, someone wondered how much higher it was possible to go. The only way to go higher is to have more speed. For that, you need a mega ramp. These look more like take-off runs for ski jumping than skate ramps. The world's largest known mega ramp is in the garden of professional skater Bob Burnquist: it is 52 metres tall.

Tony Hawk and his amazing upside-down skating skills.

Pictured here at the top of the mega ramp at the X-Games, Danny Way was always likely to be a top skater. He won the first contest he ever entered and has not stopped winning since. He has now collected five X-Games gold medals.

DANNY WAY

Most skateboarding relies on some kind of slope or ramp, but a few skaters specialize in riding their boards and pulling off tricks on flat ground. Watching an expert is a bit like watching a magician. The board spins, leaps and twists under the skater's feet. And you just cannot work out how it is done.

A skater shows off his skills at the Game of Skate tournament for flatland skaters, held at the Los Angeles Film Festival.

Early flatland

Simple flatland skills were part of very early skating. Things such as **cross stepping** on the board and doing handstands came into skating from surfing. By the 1970s, skate competitions looked a bit like dancing. Then a new style of skating, much more like today's street skating, took over. Flatland skating practically disappeared.

Flatland skating today

Under the grungy influence of street skating, flatland has made a comeback. The tricks are highly technical and hard to learn. You will probably skin your knees a few times learning these:

- hang ten nose manual – this is a rolling wheelie with the back wheels in the air and the rider's toes dangling over the nose of the board.

- one-foot nose manual to pogo – this is a one-footed wheelie with the back wheels in the air, followed by bouncing up and down on the board like a pogo stick with your foot on the truck.

- pretzel flip – here the skater does a kickflip (an ollie during which the board spins around in the air), then lands on it with his or her legs crossed.

With the back of his board up in the air, this skater performs a nose manual.

Skater Rodney Mullen is sometimes called the 'Godfather of Street Skating'. Mullen invented many of today's street and flatland tricks, including:
- the flatland ollie
- the Impossible (so-called because someone told him it would be 'literally impossible' to do)
- the kickflip (originally called the magic flip) and heelflip
- the 360 flip.

THE GODFATHER

21

Just like in surfing, longboarding is generally a more relaxed version of the sport. People ride longboards because they like the swoosh of fast-rolling, soft wheels on concrete, the motion of pumping the board through turns, and the screech of the back wheels as they slide to a stop.

Carving

One of the best things about riding a longboard is being able to carve the board through turns. The decks often have cutouts in the sides so that the board can lean over more than on a standard **set-up**. In some ways, it is more like riding a snowboard or surfboard than a skateboard.

The cut-out sides of this longboard let the rider do hard-carving turns.

Sliding stops

Stopping is not much fun on a skateboard (especially if you do it accidentally after a pebble's got caught on your wheel). But on a longboard, stopping is a hoot. Riders put weight on their front foot and push the back out, sliding the board sideways with a satisfying screech.

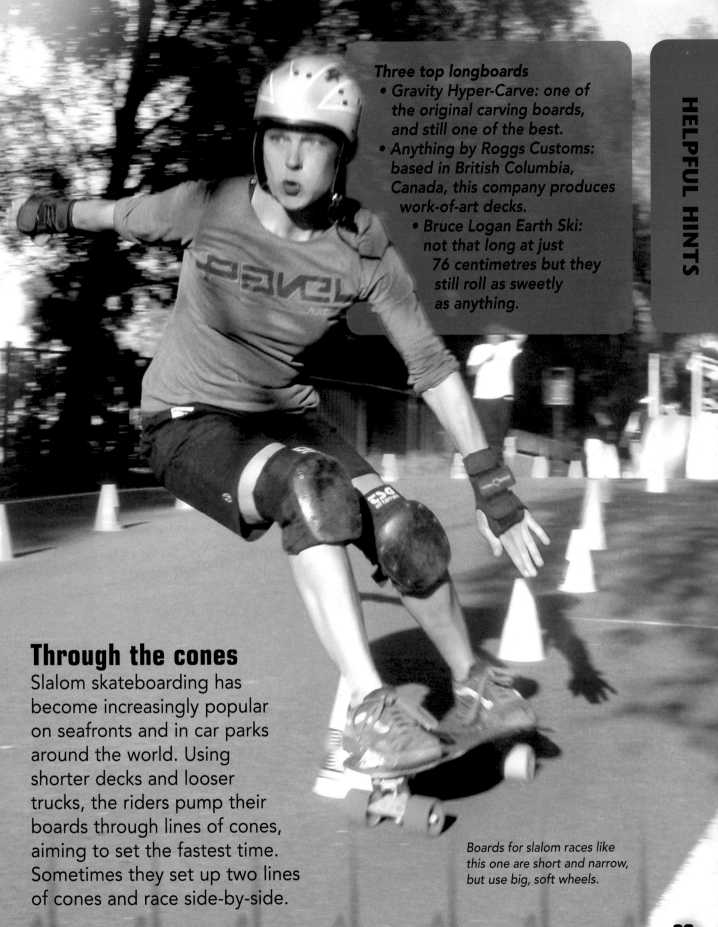

Three top longboards
- *Gravity Hyper-Carve: one of the original carving boards, and still one of the best.*
- *Anything by Roggs Customs: based in British Columbia, Canada, this company produces work-of-art decks.*
- *Bruce Logan Earth Ski: not that long at just 76 centimetres but they still roll as sweetly as anything.*

Through the cones

Slalom skateboarding has become increasingly popular on seafronts and in car parks around the world. Using shorter decks and looser trucks, the riders pump their boards through lines of cones, aiming to set the fastest time. Sometimes they set up two lines of cones and race side-by-side.

Boards for slalom races like this one are short and narrow, but use big, soft wheels.

23

Downhill racing is a spin-off from the longboarding scene, and has recently become increasingly popular. You might not immediately realize that the riders are skaters, though. They tend to be dressed up in motorbike leathers to keep them safe in high-speed crashes!

Downhill racing

To watch, downhill skateboard races are like a cross between **luge** and **boardercross**. The racers push out of a start gate, then get into as low a crouch as possible. They use long, fast-rolling boards, and swoop side-by-side down a winding course. Usually they race on a steep, closed-off road. Crashes are common, which might be why downhill races have started to attract increasingly large crowds.

Downhill racing requires intense concentration, as you can see from these riders' faces.

IGSA World Championships
The IGSA is the International Gravity Sports Association. It runs the downhill skateboarding World Cup. Contests take place all round the world, and the overall winner is whoever scores the most points in the whole year. In 2011, events included:
- *Maryhill Festival of Speed, USA*
- *Kozakov Challenge, Czech Republic*
- *Insul Cup, Germany*
- *Padova Grand Prix, Italy*
- *WinSport Canada Cup, Canada*
- *US National Championships, USA*
- *Talarrara Pro, Brazil*
- *Newton's Nation, Australia*
- *Hot Heels Africa, South Africa*

This speed skater has got down into a streamlined crouch to minimise air resistance so that he goes even faster.

Return of the snake

Snake runs are long, swooping paths down a wide concrete channel. Most of these were built in the 1970s, but recently longboard riders have started cleaning up the old snake runs and riding them again. Search YouTube for 'snake run' and it will turn up some great videos, including a few on-board ones. There is so much demand for snake runs that new runs have recently been built.

Skating is a good thing: it is fun, it gets you fit, and it stops you hanging out in a gloomy room playing computer games all the time. However, once in a while, a skater picks up a serious injury. Broken bones, paralysis and even deaths have happened because of skating accidents.

With the bowl to himself, this boarder knows he can practise moves without the danger of crashing into anyone else.

Take precautions

It pays to take a few precautions that will help prevent accidents happening:

Checking that your truck bolts are done up nice and tight is a good idea before every single skating session.

• use the right kit – make sure you are riding a board that is strong enough for your weight (most manufacturers set weight limits on their decks). Keep the board well maintained, and check before each session that every nut, bolt and screw is fastened up. And always wear appropriate protection – this should at least be a helmet.

• if you are going to fall off, do it right – crouch down as low as you can before falling, so that you are closer to the ground. A scrunched-up shape will also make it easier to roll, which is less dangerous than slamming into the ground. Try to relax: the stiffer you are, the more likely you are to hurt yourself.

• minimize the risks – make your skating environment as safe as possible. Sweep away rocks and pebbles that could get caught in your wheels. Never skate near cars or other vehicles, even on quiet streets.

> **Ramp rules!**
> Riding a ramp can be especially dangerous because of the speeds involved. Skaters have developed a set of rules for ramp-related behaviour:
> • Always wait your turn on the ramp, and never cut across another skater.
> • While waiting, stand back from the top of the ramp – otherwise you might interfere with whoever is riding.
> • Give people a bit of encouragement if they pull off a new trick. Most people do this by whooping, or banging the tail of their deck on the floor.

The world is littered with top skate spots – almost every town or city has somewhere that is good to ride. But where would you head for if you won the lottery, and could pack up your board and travel anywhere in the world? Here are a few suggestions:

BaySixty6, London, UK

London is a big skater city, but BaySixty6 is its only indoor park. On a wet day, you are guaranteed to see some hot skaters in action here.

Encinitas YMCA, California, USA

Home to one of the most famous vert ramps in history, this park has featured in hundreds of videos, magazines, adverts and posters.

Kona Skatepark, Jacksonville, Florida, USA

Skate a bit of history by visiting this park, which was built in the mid 1970s. It is home to one of the best-known and most amazing snake runs in the world.

Millennium Park, Alberta, Canada

Open 24 hours a day and free to get in, Millennium Park is said to be the world's largest outdoor public skate park. One of the few new snake runs to be built since the 1970s has recently been added.

Stapelbäddsparken, Malmö, Sweden

A huge park, in a city that is not far from the Arctic Circle. In summer, you can theoretically skate until 11 o'clock at night, then start again at 3 o'clock in the morning. (Of course, that does mean it is dark most of the time in winter, but the ground is covered in snow anyway.)

Stapelbäddsparken in Malmö has an area just for skateboarders (above). The huge park is dedicated to all kinds of urban culture, including art and music.

Woodward West (California) and Woodward East (Pennsylvania), USA

Less pure skate parks than training camps for skaters of all levels. Most of the instructors are pro skaters who spend a few weeks each year passing on some of their skills to Woodward students. If you want to move your skating up a level or two, this is a good place to go.

Other skaters look on as a young ripper practises transitions at Camp Woodward.

PlayStation.2

WOODWARD
www.campwoodward.com

900

trick in which the skater spins through 900 degrees (two-and-and-a-half turns) while airborne.

boardercross

rough-and-tumble snowboarding event in which four riders race each other down a course featuring jumps and turns.

crew

group of skaters who often skate together.

cross stepping

surfing skill that involves walking sideways along the board by crossing one leg over the other.

fakie

backwards.

grinds

tricks involving sliding part of the board along an obstacle, for example a wall or handrail.

landing

successfully completing an aerial trick.

luge

winter sport in which the rider slides down a hollowed-out course, face-up and feet-first.

ollie

trick in which the skater jumps the board up off the ground.

ripping it up

skating really well and aggressively.

set-up

another name for a skateboard, usually applied to one where the skater has picked out the individual parts and put them together.

slamming

hitting the ground hard.

traction

grip.

turned pro

became a professional, which means being paid to do something.

vert

short for vertical. Vert ramps are ones with vertical sides.

Competitions

Probably the biggest skating contest in the world is the X-Games, which is organized by the ESPN sports television channel. There are both summer and winter X-Games, and as well as the original US-based versions, there are now contests in Europe. The Summer X-Games features skating contests for big air, vert ramp, best vert trick, street and park skating. Catch up with the latest contests, skater biographies and videos at www.espn.go.com/action/blog?sport=xgames.

Details of the IGSA Downhill Skateboarding World Cup can be found at www.igsaworldcup.com, as well as world rankings and lists of past champions.

Organizations

The world governing body for skateboarding is the ISF, or International Skateboarding Federation. Its World Championships are part of the Dew Tour, a North American series of extreme-sports events. You can find out more about the ISF at www.internationalskateboardingfederation.org, and more about the Dew Tour at www.allisports.com/dew-tour.

Trick names

www.board-crazy.co.uk/tricktionary.php
Do you know your 50-50 Caspar from your 50-50 Truckstand? This site has excellent, clear explanations of these and hundreds of other skateboarding trick names. There are also some really good free instructional videos.

INDEX